Living And Healing
Through Horses

Living And Healing Through Horses

Finding and harnessing the magnificent strength and healing powers of the Horse.

Eileen J. O'Connor

To order additional copies of this book, contact:
Xlibris Corporation
1-888-795-4274
www.Xlibris.com
Orders@Xlibris.com
90869

DEDICATION

I would like to dedicate the book to my Dad,
Thomas W. O'Connor.

CONTENTS

INTRODUCTION

Is it love at first site for you with Horses? It was with me. Do you slow down to look even if you own your own horse or have been riding forever? Have you ever been pulled over for speeding while daydreaming about horses? It can happen very easily when you lose yourself to the horse.

Horses have an amazing ability to share with us our humor, sadness, successes and compassionately touch our own ability to grow and thrive. In this book, that power is touched upon and the physical and emotional power of the horse is shared in hopes that you find that bond yourself.

I never could have expected how much horses would go on to teach me about life and my part in it. If you let them, horses can have a profound impact on our self will, the development of our inner courage and our ability to be empathetic while remaining strong and grounded. Horses are by far the most magnificent of all creatures and to me the best of the animal teachers.

The bonds I developed and enlightening experiences I have had through horses began with my very first pony ride to eventually competing and showing horses professionally. I decided to move to Southern California and experienced the beautiful landscape of the West Coast by horseback, always in awe of the true beauty of horses in the most breathtaking settings of the mountains and sea in Malibu. I am very fortunate to be riding, teaching and continuing to learn every day more and more about horses, as I take their strength, courage and serenity and weave that force into my life in order for me to grow and live.

Within the pages of this book, you can start to encounter and build that special bond with horses as well as living and healing from the horse. Give yourself a chance to grow and connect with the horse, it will be the best experience and most beneficial animal relationship you may ever have.

This book is a story of what I have learned and important points that are not always stressed when you learn about horses and learn how to ride. It also goes on to share the ability of the horse to empower us and how they have over the course of my life always provided a constant source of strength and support. There has never, and I can truly say never a day so far that I have gone to see my horse or go on a ride and I felt worse than before I went to go ride. I'm not going to include trips to the hospitals with that thought, but that is probably the only exception. I feel very fortunate and blessed that I am able to have horses in my life and such a passion for riding horses within me that it remains a constant in my daily life.

CHAPTER 1

Horse Therapy

Even before the domestication of the horse, horses were looked at as majestic beings. Horses are sensitive and fascinating animals that are easy to get to know and quickly bond with people if presented a kind, teaching and loving environment. Horses respond to kindness and understanding in the way dogs do, but in as much as I love dogs as well, it is a different almost unexplainable trust that you build especially with your own horse. Riding a horse alone is quite an experience. Riding a horse of your own for years as the horse goes through all your lives ups and downs listens to you on trail rides, loses and wins with you at shows, spends long night while your sitting in the stall with them and having some of the best Sunday morning breakfasts together, having the vet come up for a scary bout of colic. Horses become fascinating friends and we depend on them for our sanity and to find our own way of balancing the realities of life and relationships while having that fairy tale character, our horse remain our one strong, loving, kind yet dangerous support for us among none other. Horses have always been a strong backbone for me, I have depended on their strength in so many ways to push me through and make me stronger and many times I was not riding them when they helped me the most. Therapy through horses is a fine way of becoming a stronger, more independent and better person. You must of course, start with yourself and the horse. Always remember to respect their size and capacity for creating a very dangerous situation. With that in mind, horses can show us view into the world we may never have had the opportunity to see without bonding with them and giving them the opportunity to teach us.

CHAPTER 2

History of the horse

The classification of the post-glacial old world horses available that were first documented are not even spoken of as species, but as kinds of horses or "types".

The first being Ewart's celtic pony better called the Atlantic pony. The modern breeds resembling this strain are the Exmoor and a certain strain of Icelandic.

The second Ewart's Norse horse and inhabiting northern Eurasia. Modern breeds mostly resembling it are the Norwegian Fjord pony a certain type of Highland pony and the Noriker heavy horse of the sub-Alpine region.

A third and spoken of horse not pony with a Central Asian habitat. Is the Akhal-Teke of Central Asia and the Karabakh both of which are a golden dun color. This ancestor of the Nisaean and Bactrian breeds and to the extend 50% through the Turks the Bactrian and the Andalusian of the Thoroughbred.

The fourth a pony sized horse of western Asia the modern breed resembling it is the Caspian pony. This latter is thought to be a handful of allied breeds found chiefly in Persia. But in part this type is bred into a multitude of domestic races endowing them with many qualities including being beautiful.

The only natural enemy of the horse is man.

CHAPTER 3

Horses in the Wild

The mustang horse is a symbol of the American West. The mustang and the Galiceno pony of Mexico descend from Spanish stock introduced to the American continent by the conquistadores in the 16th century. Mustang is a corruption of mestena, meaning a group of or a herd of horses, and is used to refer to the wild or semi-wild horses that used to roam in great numbers in the western states. The Galiceno, originating in Galicia in northwest Spain was introduced into the US during the 1950s and was officially recognized as a breed in 1958.

To talk of the Mustang as a free, wild horse is a thought that comes to mind of most Americans. In reality, the Mustang breed is and has been in jeopardy for quite some time. The majority of these mustangs survive in what are called refuges in the western states. At the beginning of the 20th century, there were an estimated one million wild horses. However, organized killing to supply pet food and meat for human consumption had reduced the mustang and its offspring so badly that in 1970 the Mustang was protected by law as an endangered species. In 1957 one of the first mustang protection groups was started by Robert Brislawn, a Mustang breeder. He tried to preserve the purest of possible strains of early Spanish horses of the barb and andalusian type. The American Mustang Association was formed in the 1960s and helped to not only preserve but promote the Mustangs through an intelligent breeding program. The Spanish Barb Breeder's Association, formed in 1972 with the aim of restoring the true Spanish Barb like those of the 15th and 18th centuries. The height of a mustang within that true breed is about 14h.

Much is being done to protect and provide adequate resources for these wild horses and burros. The Bureau of Land Management has a huge task on its hands and while it has government funding, it cannot begin to take on the amount of wild horses and provide the exact perfect situation for these horses alone.

If you want to help or just learn more of their plight, go online to the BLM Wild Horse Programs and there are vast amounts of information to be found. It is worth your while to research like any organization and talk to the proper authorities of ways to help these beautiful pieces of our American history.

Federal protection and a lack of natural predators have resulted in thriving wild horse and burro populations that grow substantially each year. The BLM monitors rangelands and wild horse and burro herds to determine the number of animals, including livestock and wildlife, that the land can support. Each year, the BLM gathers wild horses and burros from overpopulated herds in places where vegetation and water could become scarce if too many animals use the area.

These excess animals are offered for adoption to good homes and qualified people through the BLM's Adopt a Wild Horse or Burro program. After caring for an animal for one year, the adopter is eligible to receive title, or ownership, from the Federal government. While the challenge of adopting out enough animals is greater than ever, the program is a popular one. In fact, the BLM has placed more than 225,000 wild horses and burros into private care since 1971.

For more information on BLM adoptions, please visit their adoption schedule. To apply to adopt a wild horse or burro on-line, please go to the BLM's site for an application you are interested in adopting directly from one of the BLM's holding facilities, please visit the agency's page called facilities.

Can't adopt but still want to help? The BLM's Wild Horse and Burro Program gets thousands of calls from people that cannot adopt but still want to help the mustangs and burros. You can be a volunteer, serve on advisory committees and if possible donate money to assist wild horses and burros.

The above information was taken directly from the BLM website.

CHAPTER 4

Where Did Horseback Riding Come From?

The first definitive records of man riding a horse date back to 1600BC and are depicted on the tomb of Lorena of Egypt. From long before this however there are plaques still in existence that show man sitting on the quarters of a nagger (write in the definition). This horse-like animal is now rear but was in fact domesticated long before the horse. The next recorded horsemen of any note were the Assyrians great hunters of the 800s BC. They sat in the centre of the horses back as opposed to perching on his quarters and were in turn followed by the Persians. But it was a Greek calvary officer Kenophon who

provided the first landmark in classical equitation.

Born in Athens in 430 B.C. Kenophon's two books Hippike and Hipparchikos provide a wealth of information on a system of riding that is just as applicable today as it was when it was written and with formed the base of the classical equestrian art. They cover breaking buying and schooling young horses and Kenophone trained his horses in most of the movements that we know today. As well as balancing and suppling exercises involving changes of pace and direction turns and circles he also taught his horses to jump collectively off their hocks and enjoyed hunting and cross country riding when he was able to put his manage work into practice.

Xenophon also took the time to study the horses mind. He believed in a system of reward and correction for if you reward him with kindness when he has done what you wish and admonish him when he disobeys he will be most likely to do what you want. This holds true in every branch of horsemanship (unless you take kindly to the teachings of the newly claimed versions of natural and unknown gypsy like horsemanship training) that can be found for a high price because of its newly claimed success in the horse industry. I don't believe in it and don't recommend and will always prefer a simple and direct approach with horsemanship. Surprisingly and although his techniques proved to be efficient and above the scale of horse knowledge at the time Kenophon did not ride with a saddle only bareback. He rode with a long leg and a turned down toe maintaining that man's naked leg gave a greater degree of adhesion to the horse's sweating coat if the two were in direct contact.

There led to the invention of the saddle as in battle without one often proved deadly. The invention of the saddle built high at both pommel and cantle was initially used by a group of Nubian mercenaries from the Nile valley that the course of mounted warfare was changed. This high cantle provided a base against which the mounted soldier could brace his back when closing the bodies of infantry. The invention of the stirrup first used by the Huns of Mongolia in the fourth century AD the use of the Horse advanced rapidly although we know little of the use to which they were used for in the Dark Ages that followed.

The Middle Ages however saw the beginning of Charlemagne's Age of Chivalry with jousts and tourneys between teams of knights and who initially at least rode light Arab or barb type horses and wore light chain mail. The journey was also the beginning of an early form of musical ride or carousel which was used much later.

They rode with a long leg and their feet pushed forward. Reins held high in their left hand together with a shield leaving their right hand free to use a sword. Curb bits were much in evidence but the principal means on control was the rider's leg. The end of the mounted knights came as more and more armor and what we call today as tack was placed upon the horse thereby causing him to be slow and unable to turn and move throughout the battles providing him incapable of good defense and therefore a sitting duck on the battlefield. It did however establish riding and a newly favored forward seat riding with a looser rein on Arab type horses. Riding was first recognized as an art form in its own right on an equal footing with the classical arts of music painting literature and so on in the period of 1500-1600 to the point that a nobleman who did not have an education in that days horsemanship and equitation was not considered completed.

Today's dressage was formed throughout this period of knights performing the pirouette piaffe and passages forming the basis of the work on the ground, while the levade courbette and the capriole formed the basics of the airs above the ground. Elegant Baroque riding halls of which the last remaining one is the Spanish Riding School in Vienna built in 1735 by Fischer von Erlach although first built of wood in 1572 prior to that the area it covered was laid out as a training ground in 1565). Sprang up all over Eroupe to house the stately carousels performed by members of the aristocracy. Kenophon and his works were rediscovered and the high School riding had begun although the horses were initially rather heavy.

Although Count Cesare Fiaschi's book written in 1559 advocates like Kenophon the use of patience when dealing with horses and recommends the use of hands legs and voice used in combination it appears his rather cruel and unusual methods such as using hot sticks to ask the horse to go forward and tying hedgehogs and cats to the horses tails were as well methods he deemed appropriate for his desired results. He did use more natural aids as what we call the "cluck" of the human voice today as well as artificial aids using the bridle and a mild jointed bit with no curb chain acting on the bars of the mouth and without any port. His best known student and successor Frederico Grison who takes the credit and is usually called his first master, he taught in Naples and his book Gli Ordini de Cavalcare published in 1550 may well be the reason for this claim to fame. Whatever the reason his popularity spread and was translated into English by the instructions of the Queen Elizabeth 1.

Along came Grison's success Giovanni Baptista Pignatelli who also taught at the Academy of Naples and incorporated some circus training and movements into his work. He observed in the methods of the circus performers that although a high degree of obedience and balance was necessary from their horse's physical force achieved by mechanical means and sever bits was not employed to get the desired result. He was not slow to see the advantages in this form of riding and training and gradually using some of the circus methods the whole picture of classical riding took on a lighter appearance and many of the more severe aids were abandoned. Horses of a lighter Spanish build became popular and to keep with the demand for this type of horse studs were set up the best known being the stud at Lipizzaner it was founded with nine stallions and 24 mares in 1580 by the emissary of Archduke Charles the Freiherr von Khevenhiller and it established the breed which we now know as the Lipizzaner.

CHAPTER 5

Domesticated Horses

Although horses seemingly enjoy their time with humans, many of them take a long time to get there. A stabled horse is way out of its comfort zone in comparison to a wild horse. There is no way you can take a wild horse and then treat it like a horse that has been born a domestic horse.

Many people assume that their wild traits such as finding food and water and/or fitting in well with other horses when turned out in a field together or as a herd is an easy transition for the horse. It is not and shouldn't be treated like it is. Keeping that in mind, it is important to re-iterate the basic facts of horse care, they need to be fed properly, groomed and exercised. They must be kept in a thriving environment, not just existing and getting by. If you are not in a position to provide this type of basic care, you are not in a position to have your own horse at this time.

Horses are naturally nervous animals and often times don't adapt easily they should always be treated as individuals.

Horses even though they are domesticated and their association with man dates back some 5,000 years, few will instantly trust a person. All horses are easily frightened by things they do not understand, are not clearly visible or make loud or unfamiliar noises and sounds. If in your beginning relationship with any horse, you can build some type of trust and they know you are the provider of their food and they can trust in you to provide some kind of assurance and reliability, then you have begun a good, stable relationship with the horse. Horses often look to you to make major decisions, such as whether or not to go forward. That is one of the simplest issues with the horses is whether or not to go. It can be something as easy as moving past an object, going through a puddle or just being placed in a different stall. Your confidence and re-assurance to the horse will usually result in both of you working as a team. Often, a relationship where trust is mutual for you and your horse takes a bit of time. But, just understanding that although he is big and appears powerful and sometimes very secure horses are by nature timid and insecure animals and need you to help them along the path toward their self confidence.

I have had many different horses of my own. A horse that was in fact the stereotypical type, i.e., a four year old, thoroughbred gelding off the race track that should have been hard to handle and difficult to re-train. He was one of the easiest and quietest horses I have ever handled. I was riding him on the trail and down the town's roads within one week. He was a very sweet horse, unfortunately I had to sell him due to some circumstances, but he went to a great home and is now used for therapeutic riding and lessons.

By spending time with all different breeds of horses, it is much like spending time in a building full of different people. You get to know them one at a time. Horses are by nature a nomadic, grazing animal. They want to be able to roam and move around. They don't necessarily run fast all around their paddocks all day, but often times stay in a small area and walk around now and then throughout the day. This is true of domesticated horses as well.

CHAPTER 6

Your own Horse!

Ask yourself this question; What is it about a horse that makes me want one of my own so much? Your reasons are always going to seem like the best ones to make decisions with. They come from your experiences and life journeys. They can be impulsive, or they can be the best planned and thought out reasons, but, both of these reasons or decisions can have either dire or positive consequences, as we all know. But, when it comes to horses, impulsive reasons are 99.9% not going to bring a positive result and often times take a long time to fix or straighten out. I have purchased horses with every penny I had and loved these horses very much, but ended up being stressed out all the time just worrying about paying the board, paying the board late and just praying that an injury or heaven forbid the horse came down with colic. It was one of the most enjoyable times of my life, but still the most stressful. I wrote below some ways to be able to "almost" have your own horse at least until you can afford to have your own without worrying about paying for him all the time. It makes life much more enjoyable. Worrying is not fun, especially with horses and even more so if you can find a way to avoid doing it. So, I hope that the suggestions below help you in making the right decisions into horse ownership. Its is definitely one of the best long term relationships you will ever have, don't start off on the wrong foot.

Below are four great ways to become involved in horses.

Helping out/working at a stable, taking riding lessons or trail riding, leasing a horse (by the month) and of course, buying your own horse.

Hopefully, you can see from above that it may be best to use these ways in a stepping stone fashion in order to be sure that a horse lifestyle will work for you.

We are going to start this process by my assuming that you don't know too much about horses. Then, you can go from there and tailor these recommendations to match your skill level.

The first recommendation is to definitely find a stable or horse community nearby where you live or work. You don't want to have a commute to your stable. Physically go to these stables and ask around if maybe they need a little help around the barn in exchange for riding or taking a free lesson. Making phone calls or sending emails may seem easier or less intrusive, but some horse people are more likely to make a split decision of welcoming you aboard especially if you catch them on a busy morning doing stalls or rushing around turning horses out and getting ready for a busy day!

Riding lessons, lots of places, prices and personalities. All of these factors should be taken very seriously. Your instructor is the person who sets your tone of riding for the rest of your life, a strong rider is built from a strong instructor. Most importantly, a safe rider and one who will ride forever is built and shaped from a safe instructor who also rides. Key here is if your instructor only teaches (unless he or she has a disability) be wary, you want an instructor that will ride with you on a trail once in a while. You want to see what you can become and be sure that's who you want to be as a rider.

Make sure you see your instructor ride and that he/she rides often.

Horse ownership is a big **DAILY** responsibility and should not be entered into lightly, but and certainly you should have the fundamentals of horses down before getting your own horse. It wouldn't be fair to the horse or to you and you want this to be an enjoyable experience. Horses cannot be put away in a garage for the winter, they need to feel safe, be safe, fed and cared for properly and loved. Unlike a cat or dog in your own house, they need their own place. So, this doesn't come without your time or your money. Horses depend on you for their basic necessities. Therefore, if you are not in a position to get up early on a cold winter morning, and cannot clean your horse's stall because you have plans for the day, you should not buy your own horse, not just yet. In this book, I will walk you through several ways to make this dream a reality for you. As an example,

You must be creative if you are not financially able to have a horse of your own. But there is no excuse to not have at least access to them if you are willing to work at it.

You don't need to postpone your lifelong dreams of riding just because you have a family, career or other obligations. I hope this book will help you on your journey to learn as much as you can and continue learning about horses and life the horse lifestyle. Its all about chasing your dreams with horses, the more effort you put into it the more you will have to show for it.

Does anyone really know how a horse thinks? Well, how could they? But, if you have been around horses long enough and have had many experiences, good, bad, scary, funny, happy and sad, I would say you could have a pretty good idea as to how they think as a whole. I will say there is a huge difference between Mares and Geldings in the way they think and act.

First, it is important to know that whether you think your horse is smart and if he is actually smart really doesn't matter in the long run. Horses can appear as smart because they can open doors or find a way to get what they want, when other horses stay in the background. But, your horse is only using his instincts and his need for survival. Some are just better at it than others. The horse's mentality is based upon instincts and his daily need for being in a safe and secure environment. The way a horse is trained is most successful upon repetition and consistency with a reward of some sort at the end, whereby it may be a treat, a pat or praise in any form. We need to always remember that no matter how close we get to our horses, they all have that instinct and it can come out when they are hungry, angry or in pain. The horse's best defense mechanism is to move away from its threat of attack at that time. Therefore, we must not feel bad or unloved when our horses want to be with their horse friends more than us. If we get bucked off and the horse runs back to the barn and doesn't turn around to make sure we are okay, we should still be okay with that. He is just doing what is in his brain as a horse. He runs to safety. You will notice it very much among horses that are moved from barn to barn, especially those that are brought to a new barn in a pair. If that one horse is separated even if he is in a new paddock with other horses, he longs for the horse he knows. That one horse friend that makes him feel safe and secure. Although this is called the herd instinct, it doesn't mean that horses need to be in a large herd, as in the Wild West to display this inherent trait. That herd instinct in horses may not be recognized as being used in a profitable way, but that it is especially in horse racing. Racing is a simulation of the herd in flight. It is exploited for money and when the young horse is introduced to the track, it will do usually whatever it takes to keep up with the herd. He doesn't know he is winning or losing the race, he is just trying to stay safe. The same is true in a hunt, the horses jump high fences, many times resulting in accident to themselves and the riders. They are often times called crazy horses jumping over everything, when in fact, they are trying to stay with the pack. When you look at it this way it puts both those sports into the correct perspective, especially from the horses point of view. I personally believe they are not enjoying either of those sports at all.

When we look at the stable where the horse is kept and lives, it is often seen that horses feel so secure there that they run back into the barn even if it is on fire. Or, the owners cannot get them to come out in a fire. It is such a sad occurrence and happens many times in a barn fire. The horse feels safe and secure in his barn or stable. Especially if he has a run-in or a paddock adjacent to the stall for him to come in and out on his own. It provides the safe environment of a closed in and secure stall and then his freedom to walk outside in day or evening when he feels safe. The barn and stables provide food, shelter, care and represent his home, a safe (hopefully) place for him to be.

Learning about horses from the ground up, by observing them in their natural state which can just be in a paddock at a local riding stable, or by the side of the road in a big field with other horses, will give you a lot of information into how horses think and act. Observing horses if possible in their natural as in a wild horse, or otherwise known as a feral horse, maybe a trip to the land that holds these horses often owned by the BLM (Bureau of Land Management) can be the best way to understand a horse.

The most basic instinct of the horse is that of the herd. A group of horses offers a mutual safe zone, by protecting each other. A unique social system which gives each member of the herd an order of precedence ensures that harmony is maintained an although an experienced mare takes charge of the overall running of the herd, the stallion keeps order and is the main protector from routine dangers.

Many people think horses in a herd are casually roaming the landscape, taking time to graze and frolic, but just like humans, they each play an important role in the herd and work many hours at their individual jobs in order to survive.

Routine is by far one of the most important factors in having a happy, content and healthy horse. But, in the wild horses adapt their routine to where their grazing and resting can be done. The Summer can be a slower casual way of life for them as grass is plentiful, so they may graze early in the morning and late in the day. But, in the Winter there isn't much grazing its just trying to get by. So, they spent all day trying to find food. Sometimes just as it looks you may wonder how do they make it through the Winter. The truth is, many don't. Many horses starve to death in the harsh Winter and by the time the Spring and green grass comes it can be too late. But, foals are born in the Spring when the mares have plenty of grass to eat. So, they provide for their foals with healthy green grass.

EQUIPMENT AND TACK

Before beginning to ride, you must have a fairly good idea of what the tack is. It is a general term for the equipment you will be using to care for, handle safely and even more importantly ride the horse safely. The two most important pieces of tack that should come to your mind would be the bridle and saddle. But, the halter and lead rope are also tack and those are very important as well. It can be a bit overwhelming in the beginning to remember and know how to use all these items of tack, but as you handle and are around horses more often, it will become like second nature because in order to be around, ride and work with horses you need to use your tack. The basic pieces of tack are discussed below as well as some necessary safety equipment for you ride in.

Equipment for Riding

Items you should get for your own personal use that are important are your own riding helmet. Be sure your helmet is certified under the helmet guidelines for safety in horseback riding. Wearing a helmet is a must.

Riding boots with a low heel will help quite a bit as far as your positioning in the saddle and will hold your lower leg in place, something that is difficult to do especially in the beginning stages of riding. You can pick up these boots at a tack shop or go online and order them if you know you will fit into a certain size. The best thing to do is go to a tack shop and ask a professional to help fit your boots. Most employees of tack shops ride and they will know if they fit properly. You can also save some money by trying a tack or horse consignment shop in your area.

Next stage, when you know you want to continue riding and your are sure you will stay with it a pricey investment would be a pair of schooling chaps. These chaps will give you a tighter seat in the saddle. They work with the leather on the saddle to cause a gripping effect making your ride safer and more pleasurable due to less sliding around in the saddle. These should be worn all the time, you can even wear them over shorts!

As you ride more often and feel as though this is something that has become your passion, you may want to get your own riding saddle. Western or English, this is quite an investment.

The Bridle is the headgear for a horse. It consists of straps with buckles and a metal mouthpiece called a bit. The bit is used to control the animal through the reins. Bridles come in three sizes, pony cob and full and various widths. It is important for the horses comfort and your safety that this piece of equipment fit very well.

Snaffle Bridle

The snaffle Bridle is the simplest and most common with a headpiece, throat latch brownband and cheekpieces.

The double bridle is used for some forms of showing and often for dressage. It has two bits, a small type of snaffle bit called a bridoon and a Weymouth or curb bit. This bridle is the same a the snaffle bridle but it has an extra strap called a sliphead to hold the snaffle bit.

Bitless Bridle

The bitless bridle or hackamore has no mouthpiece or bit. It acts by putting pressure on the nose, lower jaw and poll, but not on the mouth The reins are attached to long cheekpieces which act like levers on the special noseband. They press against the top of the nose and lower jaw, giving the rider control over the animal Bitlesss bridles must not be fitted too low as they can interfere with the horses' breathing.

There are two other types of bitless bridles one is called a scawbrig and is very mild. It is commonly used for reschooling difficult horses and ponies that may be starting over. The next, Blairs patter design of bitless bridle is much more severe than the scawbrig. The metal shanks can exert a very strong pressure on the nose and jaw and should only be used for skilled riders. The noseband should be padded to stop any rubbing.

The bosal is a type of bitless bridle which is sometimes used western riding. It acts on the nose and jaw and it is usually made of braided rawhide. As in all bridle's they must be fitted properly in order to be able to ride the horse effectively and safely.

The most common and the original bitless bridle is a hackamore, it is mild but very effective.

ANTIQUE BRIDLE WITH TWO BITS AND TWO REINS

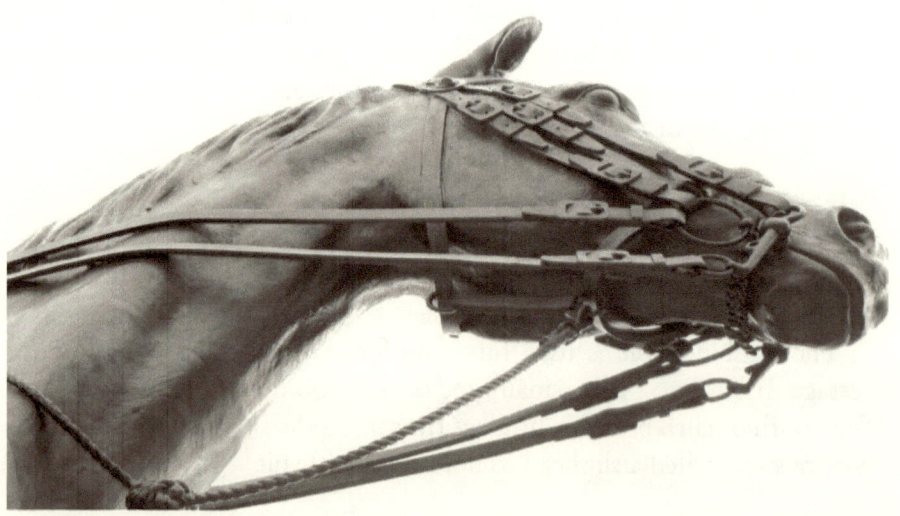

The main purpose of the bridle is to support the "bit" (the metal or rubber bar) that is in the horses mouth. The bridle is usually made out of leather and is used in conjunction with the reins as the way to control and steer the horse. The bridle is a simple piece of tack and should not be complicated with extra pieces unless they are to serve a purpose.

The most important fact about the bridle is that it fits the horse you are riding. The bit you choose to ride your horse in should always be the least severe of a bit that your horse will respond to. If you choose a snaffle bit and it works on your horse, you should try to stick with that bit. If you choose a bit that is too mild, you may not be able to control or stop your horse. If you choose a bit that is too strong, your horse may be in pain and may be dangerous in his response to the severity of the bit as in rearing or running away with you. Many horses rear in response to a too severe bit and can flip over backwards with you on them. But, the correct decision in choosing a specific bit can result in a flawless relationship with your horse. Bits and bridles create different responses and actions in your horse and it is up to you to put your horse and yourself in the best position for positive communication.

SADDLES

English Saddle

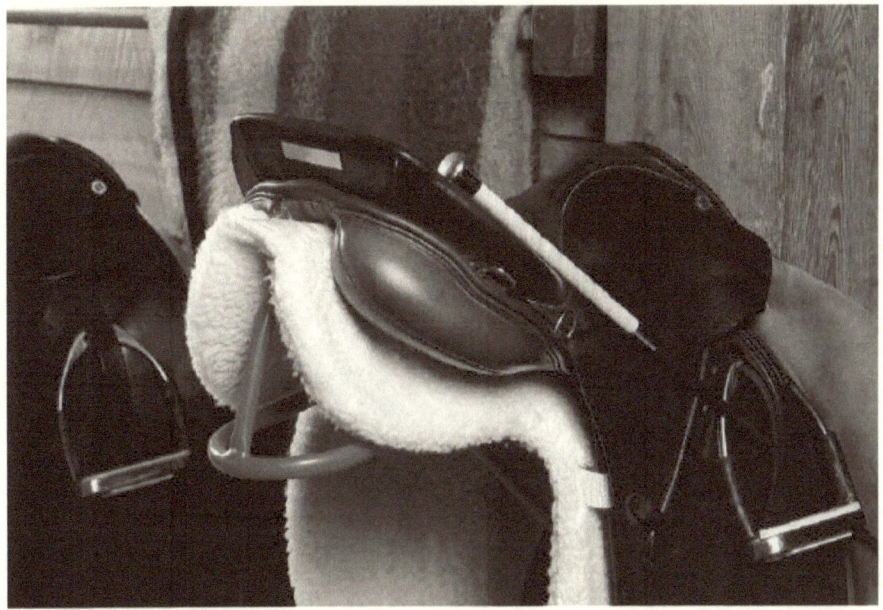

Western Saddle

CHAPTER 7

Learning to Ride

Steps to take in picking out a riding school or instructor:

1. Talk on the phone with the instructor you will be using.
2. Ask several questions, how long the lessons are, how much they cost, what the lessons consist of; i.e., how much riding time?, what the disposition of the horses are, how tall the horses are and is it a group lesson or individual lesson.
3. Cost wise, you can try to barter your prices a bit. If they say they charge $50.00 an hour, ask if you can buy 4 lessons up front for $180.00? Most instructors will say yes if they can.
4. Ask what type of a riding ring they offer and various other questions you may have. Make sure the instructor takes the time to talk to you or offers for you to come down and see the facilities. This is not only an investment for you, but a first impression and if you don't feel like its right, it probably isn't.
5. Ask about licensing, insurance and safety record. Also ask if it is a full service stable or just lessons.
6. Doing your research and having a checklist when you call is bound to help you pick a good place to start.
7. Ask about their safety routines, if someone was to fall off what is their protocol? Also, maybe get an idea of their insurance policy. If you fall off and are out of work, are your covered, etc. Did they have you sign a release? If so, you should get a copy.

If you opt to take riding lessons, you will not need to do much horse care besides the basic brushing, grooming, foot care and tacking and untacking. Basically whatever the school's system is will be the format you follow.

Tools you need are usually provided by the stable as far as brushes, tack (bridles, saddles, leads, etc.).

Mounting and Dismounting

Mounting your horse

Mounting and Dismounting are two of the most dangerous things you can do while you are horseback riding. The positioning of your legs and body in the air harnessed over the horse allow for all sorts of dangerous situations to occur.

Mounting blocks are not only safer for you, reducing the climbing on the horse, but lessen the weight landing on your horses back. Quick and easy makes things better for you and your horse.

The first thing in mounting is to face the rear of the horse and begin by taking your reins in your left hand, by having the outside rein somewhat longer, your horse will have to turn in if he starts to go forward making it safer as he is moving in and not ahead of as you climb up and on. After your left foot is in the stirrup your toe is facing right at the girth, swing your right leg over and immediately place your foot in the stirrup, sink into the saddle gently, adjust your reins and be ready for your horse to move forward. As time goes on and you are able to make progress mounting you will feel more comfortable as you get up and on your horse.

By grabbing your reins in your left hand, with your right hand, pull down your left stirrup, loop your hands, holding the reins securely in your left hand while grabbing a bit of the horse's mane, face the tail and gently place your left foot in the stirrup, turn and place your right hand, on the back of the saddle, all the while your left hand contains the reins, begin to push off of your right leg and swing, up and over easing gently into the seat. Always be aware of your reins and your horses head. Once you are seated securely in the saddle, its time to adjust the stirrups and set your hands properly with the reins.

Stirrups play an important role in riding and must be adjusted properly. Sometimes your stirrups can be uneven but feel perfect while your riding. It seems many people have two lengths of legs. In this case we are looking at one hole punch in the stirrup leather more often than not. This would not be okay if it was 2 or 4 stirrup holes different. The easiest way to check your stirrup length can be to place your stirrup up under your armpit, therefore your fingers are touching the base of your stirrup leather under the flap. Forming a straight line there will be a pretty accurate length once you get on. Of course, if someone is around to help you out, have them go in front of the horse and place your toes up close on the horses shoulder, toes in tight. This is a good head-on way to see if they are even. Also, when you do get on the stirrup should just about touch your ankle at the base, bottom of the stirrup.

Sometimes riding around for a few circles and adjusting your weight will prove to really get a feel for where they are and go from there.

Positioning your feet in the stirrup is also very important. Everything is very important. But, moving forward, place your feet so that the ball of your foot or where your toes start is a good spot for your foot to rest. Place your heels down and see if this is working for you. If your stirrups are adjusted properly, this should feel correct.

Shortly after is a good time to lift your left leg up over the saddle and tighten the girth if necessary.

REIN CONTACT

Reins are a tough subject for any new rider and they can get lost in the middle of your learning about horses. These should be recognized as the forward controls and the best way of quickly directing your horse. When you are shortening up on your reins and basically getting more control of the horse from his bit in his mouth and back to your hands. You need to be able to shorten the length of your reins quickly. This is something that you should practice until your are very good at it. It will always come in handy and when this is easy for you, it will make your riding more enjoyable.

Try placing your reins in one hand and slide (without lifting up and off the reins) down the rein until you have more contact with your horses mouth. When you are at the right point on one side, swap the reins and slide the other hand down towards the bit. Reins constantly need to be adjusted while you are controlling your horse. As time goes on and you get more comfortable, you won't even notice it and you will do this automatically and with ease.

TURNING/STEERING YOUR HORSE

Having good hands is due to experience. It all works together. Riding with your hands properly is going to pay off by regulating the pace and direction of your horse smooth and stead. You may be surprised to learn you are always adjusting even when you don't see it, you should eventually be able to feel it. It may seem that you are shortening and lengthening in micro spaces to get your horse to communicate and respond to what you want. But, whatever proper techniques you are using the end result should be clear communication.

Being the most sophisticated of the aids due to their infinite uses, they are taught and remembered by using them and getting feedback from your horses. Here are four of the rein aids.

The direct rein

This is the customarily way of decreasing or increasing the speed of your horse. Its most important characteristic is the straightness of the horses head and neck, no bending or flexion on the side. In using this rein, it can be helpful on a strong horse that is heavy in the forehand and will be effective in correcting this way of going.

The indirect rein

This is the second rein aid of importance and supplements the direct rein, controls lateral work such as bending or turning. In going from a direct to an indirect rein, the inside hand moves above and in front of the withers, or above and behind the withers, causing the horses's head and neck to bend toward the inside just enough for the corner of the horses eye to be visible to the rider, no more.

Judging the correctness of position of this rein aid is by a line from the inside of the bit through the wither bone to the horse's opposite hip. As far as its general purpose is concerned, it is most used for any two-track lateral work such as haunches-in and two tracking, or any work where the horse must bend in the same direction he is moving.

Leading or Opening Rein

This is a common way of turning and using your reins. It allows your horse to step into the turn, you open the rein to the side, never to the back and they encourage the horse to walk into or towards the open area of the rein. It is a way of encouraging the horse rather than forcing him into the turn or area you want him to go.

Neck Rein

The neck rein which of all of these is the most simple. Both of your hands move over in the direction of the turn which causes the outside rein to press against and even cross somewhat over the horse's neck. It is not surprising that this is used mainly in western riding as it is easy to do with one hand. It is a great tool and if your horse can neck rein and ride with the other rein aids, you can have much better communication with him.

Rein contact is always a dispute among instructors. I suggest riding with a rein forming a straight line from the horse's mouth to your hand and elbow. This allows the firmest and most reliable amount of control of your horse and doesn't require any pulling or leaning on the reins or your hands. This is what the dispute is, you need to have control of your horse and must learn how to do this without pulling on the reins, loosening the reins on a horse, especially one you are not familiar with can prove to be very dangerous. There is a fine line between good hands and bad hands. Practicing is the only way to master this and like all the other learning experiences with horses, it will all pay off.

Dismounting

We have all seen the cowboys and western movie stars climb down off their horse and leave their left foot in the stirrup. This is dangerous. Once again, this positioning while dismounting can prove to be unstable and therefore dangerous and should be dealt with cautiously and patiently. Step by step. The best way to dismount is by stopping your horse and really finding a safe and comfortable place to dismount. It is almost like parking a car, be sure you are in a secure area, nothing too close to your horse or your legs, don't dismount directly in front of the barn door, as many horses will try to walk into the barn as you begin to get down. Once stopped in that safe position, begin by placing your reins in your left hand, center your body and plan to swing your leg over the back of your saddle be sure to put some effort into that swing of your right leg, not too high, but not too low or too fast. Next, lean over the saddle, double check quickly on your horse's position, be sure to make him stand and slide down. I always remind people to be careful if you have buckles or zippers, on your coat or shirt. I have scratched many saddles while dismounting and some never recovered. Stopping at this point you will be almost standing with your left foot still in the stirrup and your right leg beside it. Remove your left foot from the stirrup and slide down gently and slowly all the while maintaining the contact of your horse in the reins in your left hand. Immediately Step away from the horse as they sometimes walk forward at this point and quite often this is a good time for them to accidentally step on your foot. Put the reins over his head and walk him forward quietly. Try to refrain from letting your horse rub his head all over you and/or eat grass immediately after you dismount. A good head scratch once in the barn with the bridle off and some grazing in a field or treats with his halter on are not only safer, but teach him to be polite.

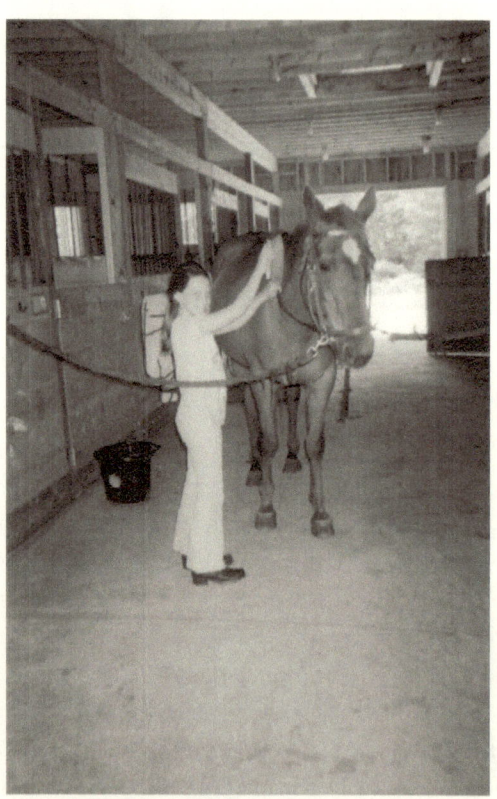

Walk

The walk of course is the horses first and slowest gait. Once mounted on the horse, begin moving forward by keeping your eyes and chin up, shoulders back and hips pushed forward, by bringing back the heels of your feet against the horse's sides, this encourages him to walk forward. While riding horses, forward movement is always the goal.

As you begin to ride, you will notice that it is your leg muscles that become sore first as far as parts of your body. That is because from your knees up to your waist, that area of your legs is going to stabilize and keep you in the saddle. Combining your thigh muscles and a good level of balance will help you relax and move forward with the horse's natural forward motion.

When we split up the areas of our legs and look into the area from the knees down, this adds a shock absorber to your seat and becomes the area where the horses movement can almost always be felt the strongest. This is easy to feel if you pay attention as you walk the horse forward.

First and foremost is the need to feel safe and secure in the saddle. You will at least in the beginning go through several stages of feeling secure. Once you master this feeling of security at the walk, it will surely be thrown off and have to be re-started again once you go into the next gait, the trot. This is just about growing in your riding and is completely normal to feel off balance as the horse changes its gaits.

Balance is the key word in all stages of riding, but is a goal to the new rider in order to achieve some harmonious communication with any horse you are riding. So, work on that technique at the walk and try to strive to feel balanced in your seat and with the motions of the horse as you learn all there is to know about riding. In all gaits as is the strong, direct forward movement together as a team. Even at the walk, it seems sometimes crooked or off balance. This will come natural over time as well as with other gaits. Try to observe others while walking (on the horse) riding. This can give you an idea that you are not actually moving all over the place as it may feel sometimes. Also, videotaping your riding, riding in an indoor ring with mirrors will all help ease your mind. Just stay confident and ask questions.

Walking is highly underrated. It should be done as much as you can, especially when you are new. By achieving a stable balance in your seat early on, this is surely to guarantee you a safe riding seat as you pick up your paces and go into the trot and canter.

Beginning the walk which is known as a four time pace, the horse moves each leg by itself. If you listen to his hoofs clomping, you can hear them individually. As in the trot, he moves them in diagonal pairs so it is known as a two-time pace.

As a horse walks forward, you should be giving him the ability to reach with his head, but don't allow him to get the reins pulled out of your hands. You must remember horses are tricky and will inch by inch try to get the reins away from you if they want. Not always, but keep yourself on guard for this, you are riding an animal, a big strong horse! Sitting up straight with your shoulders back, head up and legs against his side, but heels are not in his belly. A rule of thumb is heel, hip and elbow easy to remember when you are questioning your positioning. By moving forward at the walk, we squeeze together our legs, sometimes heels until the horse responds, keeping our hands quiet and reins straight. Heels stay down and our head and eyes are up. Stomach and body are relaxed but alert. Walking along, try to feel him moving underneath you and stay together with that movement. By allowing his body to move under you and you gently working with him makes it an enjoyable gait.

Transitioning back into a stop, look ahead a bit, pick a spot to stop and begin by bringing your hands back, therefore pulling on the bit in his mouth, just gently enough also sinking your seat deep into the saddle, exhaling as this is performed. The horse should come to a halt and stand still, if he his pulling or backing up, check your leg positioning and make sure your legs are not on him and you are not pulling back too hard on his mouth, which would be asking him to back up. There are many fine lines in riding, once you get these down it will be easier and more enjoyable.

Trotting

The next gait after the walk is the trot, don't rush into it. As you walk, think of asking and urging your horse to follow into the next gait of the trot. As you begin the trot it will feel bouncy and rough. You should start out in a western saddle if there is one around, this will give you additional confidence as it will help with your balance. Your balance must be in order to begin posting and trotting confidently.

As you ask the horse to ride using your legs, press them firmly against his sides, as he begins to trot you will sit a few beats then rise gently up and out of the saddle. The horse trots by moving his left foreleg and right hind leg at the same time and his right foreleg and left hind

eg. together as well. This is the bouncing you are feeling. It's time to learn how to post. You will soon learn to time your posting so that as you rise out of the saddle, it will coincide with your horse's upward bounce. Only your knees and legs, particularly the inner thighs should be absorbing the shocks of your horses driving legs.

Think of lifting and lowering as you post. Look down at the outside shoulder of the horse, when it is up, you should be out of the saddle, just slightly, sit back down and rise up again. Try this constantly at the walk, until you get it. Then proceed at a sitting trot (not posting) relax your inner core muscles (abdominals) breath in and out as your ride and have someone on the ground watching and helping you, preferably a licensed instructor. Once you pick up posting you won't forget and believe me, this is a good thing to learn and move forward from. Be sure you have it down before you go into the canter, as well as some good balance.

Canter

The canter is the gait we all wait for when learning to ride, some call it a gallop, but it's a canter. A gallop is after the Canter and is faster than the canter. The Canter is much smoother and more like a rocking chair feel to it when done correctly. It may even feel slower than a trot and definitely more manageable than your experience in the beginning with trotting.

You want to begin cantering by relaxing your muscles, as your body is to work with the horse and the end result is to become one forward motion together. As you ask the horse to canter, we try to work with leads. Think of a lead as a signal in asking the horse to canter. The best way is to go directly from the walk, the horse may almost pop up into the canter, but this will become natural for you as far as your balance and the way it feels.

You will be leaning forward more at the canter, if just so slightly than at the trot. As usual hold your hands apart and in front of you. Keep your arms, hands and reins in a straight line from your elbow to the bit, but let them give and take with your horse's head motion. Shorten the reins so that you always have control and can pull him up if you need to. Keep your legs in the usual heels down pressed against the saddle position.

Horses canter by moving forward one foreleg (that will become the lead leg), then the other foreleg and the diagonally opposite hind leg, and then the other hind leg.

The first foreleg to strike out is his lead. Leads are important because the help to balance him, if he is not on the correct one (the inside lead), in a small circle, he can fall in and put so off balance that he will fall down on the ground obviously with you on him, ouch!.

Therefore to support that weight, keep your inside leg on his inside helping him to push his hindquarters away from the pressure and keep his balance.

The simplest way to put a horse on his lead, i.e. get him to canter is to point him in a clockwise direction around a ring. Turn his head (his nose), to the right and push forward using your weight, lean forward a bit (sitting in the saddle) and use your left leg all of it from your knee down firmly even with a small kick into his belly to almost pop into the canter. Most horses respond to this first time (if they are trained). Then you will push with your body weight ever so slightly for him to continue that canter, keep your head up and urge him forward. They do hesitate when you give in or slack off, so keep him moving, and always forward.

Bring him back to a trot, sit to this trot and gently ease him back into a walk.

The Serenity in Horsebackriding

Especially for women, we have a tendency to rely on our partner to fulfill our desire to be completed. We intuitively are caretakers and protectors. But, when we feel that loneliness does not go away although we are doing our share of caring, loving and protecting, it may be something that no one else can fulfill. That emptiness needs to be filled from within.

Connections in all forms of life give us fulfillment and hope. Often times that can be difficult to search for and we start to assume that it is either not available to us or out of reach, that is only for successful people. I don't mean financially successful people only. Just when we see people with a certain calmness and look of acceptance in them, we wonder how they got like that. In order to bring yourself to a comfortable place in your life and actually be able to get along with yourself, we need to be able to trust. Trust in your future, your thoughts, believes what you believe and trust that you should always be on a transforming journey of yourself all your life.

Horses come in to play with this notion because they live like this 24/7. They do not live in chaotic lives, wondering what step to take next, letting other horses ruin their lives, hanging out with bad horses and not moving on. Humans do this and it's for reasons of fear, insecurity or other damaged areas of their emotional well being.

When horses and people combine their outlooks and experiences and go forward, as an example of a new young girl buying her first pony. This pony may or may not have ever shown before; the girl may be a young, slightly novice, and definitely nervous rider. But, together, they both crave love, affection, attention and acceptance. So, they become stronger together. They do go on to win shows, lose shows and be okay with the outcome because they are bonded as a team. Their chances of success both out of the ring and for the child in school have just improved greatly. As we know it would be best if they could stay together and go forward together as well.

An inmate out west on a jail horse training program (which they have with the mustangs), may be totally lost due to his incarceration, poor family life, drug and alcohol abuse, lack of education and/or other numerous bad choices, he may also be an inner city person, with not many animal skills, most definitely not horseback riding and training. On the other hand, this mustang is probably off the range, scared, dying to get back to his freedom somewhat like the inmate and does not have the tools to do anything about it. So, although this sounds like a disaster waiting to happen, you may be pleasantly surprised as once they connect, they find the same in each other. With some basic training on both parts, they should be able to relate to each other and bring out their insecurities at once. The next step is a bond so strong because they now rely on each other for support. These two should in the horse world make a great team. This doesn't always happen with people and it's a beautiful thing. I love horses so much that I am always pro-horse. I also believe in them and their ability to heal and change people that want to be changed. They have a huge capacity for love and to be loved.

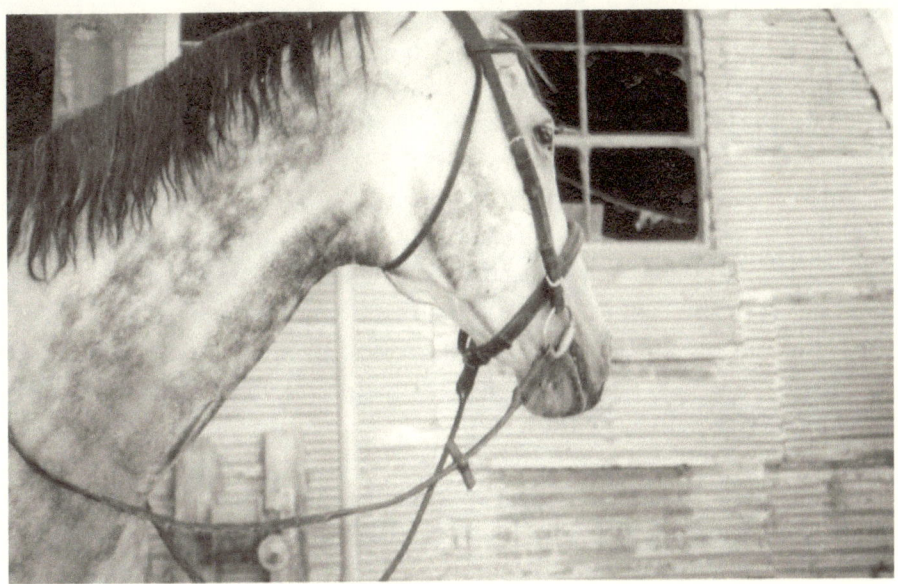

When you ride a horse you must think forward. No matter what. It is almost like being one step ahead naturally. This is how it works. So, there is a magical occurrence when two come together from different worlds and remarkably move forward to be better than they would have been alone or on their own.

Horses are great communicators, all we have to do is listen. As a prey animal, he is always on guard. Therefore, he is very sensitive to what may be, doesn't always have to be a threat, or a sign, signal. When you communicate and hold back, he knows you may want something from him so as to come over to you, but are fearful. He may just come on over anyway. They also help you to read into dealing with people not just horses, overcoming your fears of confrontation in a healthy way. Horses share a great sense of self-awareness and peace from within. They want to be happy. Since they cannot speak, they must become the best at communicating with people in a way that works. They depend on people for their food, shelter and livelihood.

When you work with horses and try to work on yourself at the same time, the results are very rewarding. You will discover patterns that used to stop you in your tracks, and find ways of pulling that inner confidence out and being able to use it once your horse therapy is over into your outside life.

Horses have been know to help people with past abuse issues, low self-esteem, aggression, self-doubt, depression and overcoming many of life's tragic and tough obstacles within themselves.

Horses are very therapeutic in so many ways. But this is an example for the horse to help you or your loved ones to get through many obstacles that you just can't seem to figure out with other forms of therapy.

Being involved with horses even just brushing and handling them can provide you a decreased fear of failure, intimacy, the ability even bond with others, helps to take away a negative self image you may have, definitely will help decrease shyness and for many adults as well as children gives them the confidence they need to go forward in life, try new things and feel good about their choices.

Too often we miss the most important moments we experience in life, horses because they are so big and can be so dangerous hopefully force us to pay attention to them even when we can't see them behind us. Therefore, after some time spent with the horses we naturally and instinctively become more aware of our surroundings and that sense of awareness will take continue on when you leave the barn. You should be in the moment more often in your life. That is a big part of the way I have lived after being around horses for over 40 years. I notice little things, I can feel a horse behind me it almost tapes into a higher sensitivity to your surroundings and that is a nicer, safer way to live. When you live your life and are in a chaotic busy world and don't tap into your own self-awareness you miss out on a lot that life has to offer you. Through horses and other animals as well, but for me especially horses I have been able to be content and more in tune to my surroundings, thus enjoying more moments and more feelings and natural experiences in life than other people. Life is good and horses have a way of bringing out the truth in that for all of us if we give them a chance.

There is no better feeling than riding a horse you know in a beautiful place, all alone just you two and just thinking about how great your life is and how fortunate you are to be able to be there in that moment at that time!

I use these memories although I am fortunate enough to continue to make them, when I just need to remember what is important to me, yes my home life, but, the feeling of riding down that trail, particularly in Malibu looking at the ocean at the same time I see the woods and the sun and just what I think is the most beautiful place for me to be in that moment in the world and the best part of that is I'm on a horse!

These horse memories stay with you and they help you to put your life in a fabulous perspective that can't be touched with negativity and chaos. I use this a lot as I live my life on a daily basis.

There are many agencies and private companies that offer horse therapy for many groups:

Social workers
Counselors
Therapists
Probation and Parole officers

And maybe psychiatrists or other special needs programs. In addition to that there is always riding therapy for disabled children, which is a great program in itself.

These resources should be easily accessed on the internet or through your town's local newspapers or community groups.

CHAPTER 8

Next Steps—Alternatives to Buying a Horse or Best Ways to Buy One.

Once you are comfortable with being around horses and maybe you have decided to look at horses as a healing tool in your life, the next step would be to maybe get one of your own. You can do this without actually purchasing the horse. Be sure you are comfortable with the above mentioned items as well as some basic riding skills providing you to be in a safe environment while riding with the confidence you need to actually enjoy your rides as well.

You may have some horse professionals and friends at this stage try to talk you into buying your own horse, not always a good idea at this point. Try to do a lease at a friendly, people oriented, lesson, boarding barn. That way people will be around to ask questions. Its always a good idea to have others around while you are riding in case you get into any sticky situations.

Leases come in different options, half or full and then other deals can be worked out with specific owners. A half lease lets you ride 2x a week for probably ½ of the horse's board. Lots of owners will take any help with the board money, so don't hesitate to ask rather than just don't even try to lease a horse.

Many people can get a horse to ride 2x a week for $100.00 a month. Also offering to help out mucking stalls and grooming, etc. can go a long way for a few free rides.

The purpose and reason I suggest leasing is that it gives you that opportunity to actually see what its like to have your own horse. There is even more in having your own horse once you get one, like farrier bills, vet bills and just the fact that you have to be around.

But, it's a way to also have more time with one horse, you don't have to rush out of the barn after your lessons and you don't feel uncomfortable hanging around because you are leasing. I did this early on when I was about 10, my parents would lease me a horse every summer for about 4 years, it was sad when the horse went back to his farm, but my summer was great. That was also on a full lease so, it was like she was all mine.

CHAPTER 9

Horse Care

Boarding or having your horse at home. Both have the best of options. By boarding, you know your horse is being taken care of daily and things do come up that we can't predict making it impossible to get to the barn every day. But, having your horse in your backyard is one of the best experiences you can ever have. It's great for so many reasons;

Horses are always a part of your family when you have one, but when they live on the same property as you or in your back yard, it's the best! You can run out and say goodnight, tuck them in, check on them early in the morning, try to sneak in and see if they are sleeping, bring them in treats right before bed and basically just feel all the more connected to them. It is great to own a horse of your own no matter what and sometimes boarding your horse at a stable is the only way or for now the best option you have. But, when the time comes you can live with your horse at your own house it is one of the best things in the world. I worked full time and did plenty of other activities, but I never had any problems being in a hurry to drive home to see my horses. I really just couldn't wait to get home. I don't have a horse at my house now and I still love to go home, but it would be great if there was a horse in my yard as well. It is also a great feeling to know that you are feeding him, you know he has enough water, the best grain and hay, etc.

On the slightly down side of this at home stabling, if you don't have a good deal of experience, it may not be the best idea for the following reasons. If your horse gets into an accident at home, or gets loose or you get hurt, no one is around to offer assistance and if you were to get knocked unconscious, no one is there to call 911 or get help. It can also be lonely, barn friends are great, it's a very social atmosphere at the barn, you meet your friends to hang out, joke around, ride, show together, trail ride or just make new friends and learn more about horses. I loved hanging out with my friends at the barn and that is one thing I missed when I moved my horses to where I lived. Also, if you want to go away on vacation, you have to get someone you trust to take care of them, etc. So, if you have a barn at home, you may want to board your horse at first and maybe have him spend some weekends at your house until you know you can and want to take on that daily responsibility. It's okay if you don't. I love horses and still, if I could afford to board mine at a full board, inclusive stable that I trusted, I would probably do that right now. I am very busy with other jobs and school, and it would be fine with me if I didn't have to be there every single day and night. It's a lot of pressure once you commit to it. So, just be sure you take some steps in figuring this out. It isn't fun any more if you really look at getting up to feed as a chore or you have to run home right after work every night to feed and then go back out to finish whatever else you needed to do, etc.

Feeding your horse

Feeding your horse can make him a champion or it can make him very sick and even kill him. You must know how, when and what to feed your horse.

Water

One thing that I am always amazed at as I have been around several barns, is the lack of fresh water and/or many empty buckets. Most well run stables always have fresh, clean water for their horses. Many stable owners and individual owners feel as though a couple of buckets a day are okay. They seem to not be aware that they need to take the time and effort to fill their horses buckets, inside their stall and outside in their paddock. Many factors just as with us cause the horse to be thirsty, sun, heat, exercise and diet conditions.

So often I see empty buckets, dirty buckets and a plain misunderstanding about why and how much water horses actually drink and need.

I unfortunately am not surprised, but I do get very upset as to why this seems to be an issue at horse barns.

Water makes up 60% of a horses adult body weight. It is vital to his health and the functioning of his organs and blood. It is said that a horse can live weeks without food, but not for more than two days without water.

I would not ever want to be in a position to find that out. So, the quantity of water required by a horse on a daily basis is dependent on many factors, such as the weather, the size of the horse and its workload. It is best to have available to the horse at least 15 gallons of water a day (that is about three good sized stall buckets). Clean and accessible and away from an area where he could soil his own water. A stabled horse depends on you to give him clean and delicious water. If you won't drink it, don't give it to your horse. You must be aware of metals in your water in the area where you live. Often times, horses will not drink water that tastes even a bit different. So, in a case where you move from one stable to the other, it is vital that you keep track of your horses drinking behavior. Water for a horse in a stable should be in clean, rubber or plastic buckets. They should be big enough for him to get his head in and enough water in there to last him through the night.

Plastic buckets can split and have sharp edges as can metal buckets. If they fall off the wall, they can get stuck in his legs, causing him a bad injury.

I put two buckets in my horse's stall at all times, unless the middle of the Winter. During the winter I track how much he is drinking. Lack of water can cause all sorts of digestive problems, the number one and very dangerous result of not drinking enough water can be colic. During the Winter I pour warm water with a mixture of apple juice on their hay at night to make sure they drank enough water. I also feed the horses mashes with bran and lots of warm water.

Automatic water dispensers are not my first choice. I ran into situations over the years where they malfunctioned and it was hard to tell how long that had been. I know it was at least 24 hours. That happened once and so, unless you are checking them, which you should be, I feel you are relying on them too much. You may want to talk to barns that have them in place before you install them. I'm sure there are some very good ones on the market by now (2011), but seeing is believing and seeing a full bucket of water in your horse's stall may seem old fashioned, but at least it is reliable. Just reinforcing the fact, that horses need you to make sure they are getting what they need.

Watering your horse should be handled with the following important rules in mind;

1. Always provide your horse with a constant supply of clean water.
2. Always be sure he has water with his food.
3. Never work a horse hare immediately after giving a long drink.
4. After you ride, give your horse a sip of water here and there until he is fully cooled down.
5. Keep all your buckets and anything that touches your horse's water supply sparkling clean?
6. Remember how you would feel if you couldn't get any water!

A horse should have access to clean, water at all times. One exception; if your horse has been worked heavily and is hot, cool him out and then give him small amounts of water (sips) at a time, until he is cooled down. Take your time with issues like this, pre-caution is the best way of thinking when dealing with horses and a matter of minutes can make a big difference. Allowing your horse to be fully cooled down is one of the most important in avoiding any onset of colic. Colic is a digestive ailment which can come on quickly and often be deadly. Learn as much as you can about your horse's sensitive digestive system and this will help you to take great care of your horse.

Moving on to feed, horses are naturally grazers, the grass contains vitamins and minerals important to a horse's nutrition, but it does not build muscles or add fat to a horse as well as other types of feed and hay do.

Hay is for Horses!

The horse is a herbivore, that is an eater of plants and especially grass and herbs. If he was out in the wild, he would spend almost twenty hours grazing, slowly moving about looking for his food. Although their stomachs are small, they thrive on eating constantly instead of two meals a day like a breakfast and dinner. Horses that are stabled are often best fed on free choice hay, that is access to hay at either several intervals during the day 4-5 times a day or 24/7 hay.

Bad or un-nutritious hay is not fit for any Horse!

Hay is although only dried grass a complex subject among horse people. The main types of hay are listed below.

How do you tell the difference? Well, depending upon what part of the country you live in, you need to start with what you have available and what type of hay will be most plentiful year round as the horse's digestive system is sensitive.

The nutrients in your hay are vital to your horse's health. Grain stores are one place to buy hay, but if you can buy your hay from a hay farmer, that is your best bet.

Seed Hay

It is more nutritious than meadow hay. It is taken from grasses specifically sown as an annual crop, which will include the timothy and rye grass hay. This is often known as top quality hay, although it is not for every horse. Stalks and leaves are coarse. It offers a higher protein content

Meadow Hay

Has been cut from a permanent pasture and is softer to the touch and less course, often greener than seed hay. It contains a lot of different plants and is usually less nutritious and therefore is more suitable for animals in light work.

Grass Hay

Is hay that has been taken from an established pasture, it usually contains a variety of grasses and other plants with soft, thinner stalks and leaves. It offers a medium to low protein content.

Alfalfa and Clover Hay

Is a high source of protein and should be fed in small increments in order to introduce your horse to it.

These are two of the most common are alfalfa and timothy. Timothy is one of my preferences, and I feel the best hay that can be given because of its nutritional quality and digestibility. Alfalfa is good with a mix of timothy. Alfalfa is a strong hay and when fed to horses not accustomed to it can cause damaged to a horses' kidneys. So, by slowly integrating it into your horse's diet is always the best way. Always consult your vet, usually a quick phone call is all you need to know your doing the right thing for your horse, it will give you the peace of mind you need to provide the right care for your horse even if it is only a "simply question".

Different parts of the country choose to feed various types of hay. The way to find out what is best for your own horse is to ask your vet. There is not reason your horse should not be able to exist and thrive on a good quality and hay and grain diet. Supplementing when it is not necessary is like taking vitamins when you don't need them. The best way to feed a horse is simple. Good quality in consideration with his weight and exercise program.

Storing Hay

Hay continues to dry out while it is stacked, so ideally it should not be used until it is at least 5 months old. It is best eaten within 12 to 18 months.

To keep your hay usable and nutritious as it does become an investment once you buy it, store it in a dry place such as a hayloft if possible. It is best stored stacked up together, but never covered with anything that can become wet or like a plastic that would result in a greenhouse effect and cause mold.

Soaking Hay

Soaking hay is done to help with digestion. I personally soak my horse's hay in very cold months as it encourages them to take in more water at times when they risk not drinking enough due to the cold temperatures.

Dry hay and even the best of hay may contain some dust. This isn't good for your horses and to help with that, soaking your hay is the best thing to do.

The purpose of soaking in this case is to prevent dust particles and mold spores sufficiently so that they are swallowed with the hay and not inhaled though the lungs.

Inhaling this dust and possible mold spores can irritate and inflame the delicate lining of the lungs. In the past, it was recommended to soak the hay for at least 12-24 hours. This is not necessary. If you soak the hay in a big soaking bucket and go about graining and watering your horses (1/2 hour), then they hay should be ready to be fed by then. It should not interrupt a normal feed program. That way, it will be easy enough for you to do that you will do it on a regular or if you feel the need, daily basis.

Feeding Hay

Since horses naturally eat of the grass floor in the wild and while they graze, it is still okay to put your horses hay on the floor. But, you do have other options, hay nets, hay racks, etc. Keeping hay off the stall floor can help to be a good indicator of how much your horse is eating especially if he is making a mess and then ends up using it for bedding or mixing it into the shavings or dirt. It is also cleaner if he can just get the hay and not unnecessary shavings, sand (which could cause sand colic) or dirt.

Oats are still the best type of grain feed for a horse, they will get great muscle and energy. Oats are still fed at most race tracks today. It will probably cause many horses to buck and act up if fed too much of it to a family riding horse, but they will love it if mixed in with a good quality pelleted grain.

Many commercial mixtures from several manufactures are a combination of oats, bran corn, molasses and a sweet feed mix. The best quality grains are what you should feed, once again factor this into your horse budget.

Salt is another element of the horses overall healthy diet. Salt blocks should be placed on the wall of the stall for the horse to freely eat. If your horse is turned out in the pasture, you can get a large salt block that sits in a holder to be placed in the pasture.

Supplements

As with people, there are many supplements on the horse market. If you horse is healthy, eats well and you are providing him with a sufficient and good quality diet, I do not feel your horse will need any supplements. Take your time in picking out supplements and food additives if you do decide your horse may need something extra in his diet. Your best bet is to always consult with your veterinarian before changing his diet. The horse's digestive systems are so sensitive and veterinarians can give you the best advice before you make a decision.

FEEDING and GRAIN

Feeding Grain depends on two main things. How large your horse is and how much work your horse is doing.

There are so many grains on the market now that you need to consult a feed expert to be sure you don't feed your horse the wrong type of grain and definitely not the wrong amount. It usually goes by your horse's weight and should be explained on the back of the grain bags you purchase.

I do not go into detail about graining your horse because I really think that is an education in itself. As you ride your horse more and maybe in the seasons you don't ride much, your horse's needs for grain will change and should change. Due to the fact that horses can colic quickly, my best advice is to really educate yourself on this matter and talk to other people especially at your barn or if you stable at home, your vet in order to be sure your horse and you are on the same page with the graining. One thing about graining I do believe in is that horses need grain it is a very important part of their nutrition program and domesticated working horses **CANNOT** live on hay alone and be at their prime.

Veterinary Care

A veterinarian is defiantly one of the most important people you will have in your life once you have your own horse. A veterinarian can save the life of your horse by stopping illnesses before they are too serious to treat or heal.

A horse's digestive systems are extremely sensitive and the horse cannot vomit. Therefore, once a horse swallows his food, it is not coming back up, not through his mouth anyway. Colic is the most serious horse ailment and needs to be treated at once.

Horses display symptoms ranging from rolling to alleviate the pain, laying down, constantly looking at his/her stomach. Keep walking your horse on a lead until the vet arrives. A point I make in the feeding section above is that horses must have water 24/7. Dehydration can play a major role in the onset of colic. Of course, if a horse is worked heavily his water should be held back until he is cooled down.

Worming and vaccinating your horse

Horses need to be vaccinated and wormed every 6 months, usually spring and fall. Depending on where you live in the country, can depend on what your horse is vaccinated against. Check with your local vet and find out what type of schedule they recommend. Call around to be sure you are getting a reasonable price and the vaccines are necessary.

Tetanus, equine encephalitis (disease contracted by mosquitoes causing brain damage and is often fatal), are two of the shots your veterinarian can give your horse.

Worming your horse is something you can do yourself. At your local feed store they should have a variety of horse wormers. I prefer using the past wormers on the schedules the manufacturer recommends. There are daily wormers that can be placed in the feed as well, some are personal preference.

Dental Care

Even horses need dental care. Once a year you should contact a horse dental professional, otherwise known as a floater. He will come and float or file down your horse's teeth once a year. Bad teeth or sharp teeth can cause problems and interfere with your horses eating, causing weight loss and nutritional problems.

Blacksmith/Farrier

No Hoof - No Horse!

A wise statement made to indicate how important your horses hoof care is. Only a knowledgeable farrier should shoe your horse. Whether your horse is a riding pony or a top-class show jumper, his farrier is one of the most important people that comes in constant contact with your horse. Sometimes farrier's are not easy to schedule and/or get in touch with. Once you have found, through word of mouth is best a good farrier, be sure to hold on to him.

Schedule your appointment in advance if you can, every 6-8 weeks either for a hoof trim or shoes.

Be sure to be there if you can when the farrier is shoeing your horse. It is educational and important that you know how your horse acts when he gets his feet done and many questions can come up that the farrier can answer. Also, anything you can do to make the farrier's job easier is a good idea as you want to keep him around for a long time.

Shoeing a horse should never be a painful procedure for the horse. A horse should not be "ouchy" after he is shod. Lot's of horse owners especially old school owners don't like to ride their horse the day they are shod, or the next day. This is a personal decision. I wouldn't take my horse to a show that same day and I'm not sure if there is a real reason it just feels right.

But, there should not be a period of time you need to wait to ride after your horse has a visit from the farrier.

Many people opt to not put shoes on their horses, especially the back hooves. As long as your horse isn't tender that may be okay. Consult your farrier and value his opinion.

Winter shoes are an investment in safety. If you can't afford the extra expense, don't take a chance and ride if there is ice and snow. A totally barefoot horse in snow, a few inches can be safe. I prefer winter shoes on all four feet. There are many stories told of horses having catastrophic accidents slipping on ice and snow because their owner's tried to save a few bucks! Don't let that happen to you. If you live in an icy and snowy area of the country, put some money away and be sure to put winter shoes on your horse. Many farriers can reset these shoes next winter, just ask!

CHAPTER 10

Riding as an Adult

If you are the rider who has ridden earlier on in life or as a child and is now just getting back into riding, then you will want to start off slowly. A fitness program specializing in the muscles and especially focusing on core activities will help you in general and will also make riding easier to do. By working out regularly and combining that with riding, you will get the edge you need to not only be in great shape, but have the confidence you need while riding that you may have lost when you went away from riding especially if it has been a long time.

If you are a rider who is under 40 then maybe going back into the horse world is easier, because you may have kids of your own or be around them all the time for some reason. But, if you don't and want to be around people and instructors your own age which is how I would feel. I would suggest that you look into stables and just ask how old the instructor is. How much teaching experience he/she has had and ask if you could maybe watch them teach a class or just take a ½ hour lesson. I say this not because I think 40 or over is old, but because people 40 and over say that they are glad that I am their age and it seems more comfortable for them. Many young people and kids can have a know it all attitude and getting back into a sport can be intimidating and not an easy transition. If you really want to ride and don't know of a great stable to get into right off, then you may want to prepare to go through a couple. That is why I strongly suggest a fitness program on top of your riding lessons. It makes things so much easier and you will have the energy to ride at a posting trot, confidently handle your horse and feel refreshed after a ride, hopefully not wiped out or exhausted. These horses you will be riding may be strong and you want to be able to control them especially in an emergency. I suggest that you don't go into the stable with the attitude that you are overly experienced. Not because you don't have a lot of experience, but because if you haven't ridden in a while it's nice to start off on a calm, easygoing school horse. A nice gelding that they use for beginners is the best way to go. After you are confident again at the walk, trot and canter, maybe you can go up a level to a more challenging horse to ride. After teaching for over 20 years, I have had quite a few students over the age of 40 that decided to ride again. It's great! I love teaching these students. But, I tell them to follow the advice above to get the best result and have the most fun. Often times, I am the second or third instructor they have found and along with that goes stories of disappointment, dangerous accidents or mishaps and a lot of almosts that didn't go forward with their riding because they were led to believe that they didn't belong back in the saddle or they were given horses that were "too much for them" at that moment and fell or just got scared. I really don't like hearing those stories because its terrible. Everyone should have the opportunity to ride or get back into riding and it should never be a scary or disappointing experience. Starting any sport later on in life has its own set of challenges. I tried skiing and gave up quickly. Perhaps if I had started when I was a kid, like with horses I would enjoy it, but with persistence and practice and allowing the horse to give you some of their strengths, you can definitely learn to ride at any age and enjoy it.

If you keep looking and trying different horses and meeting new horse people it will pay off. You have to be specific, look for a barn where you can learn and you would feel comfortable boarding your horse or leasing your horse from them if you were to hopefully get your own horse at some point in the future. That way, you can stick around, learn, make some friends and always feel like your horse will be safe there. It is so important to feel comfortable when you get into the barn and driving down the driveway you don't want to feel like you don't want to go to the barn that day.

Always make sure you have the right attitude and keep an open mind when you are riding, don't be afraid to try new techniques as long as you feel safe, go with your own instinct all the time as far as safety goes and remember you are riding for a purpose, so get up there enjoy every ride and make your life better because of it.